"Those who become Christians become new persons. They are not the same anymore, for the old life is gone. A new life has begun!"

2 Corinthians 5:17 (NLT)

This workbook is based on the discipleship packet developed by Russ Akins, president of Master Plan Ministries. Russ taught these principles during thousands of discipleship appointments and trained many Christian workers to share their faith and make disciples. His Great Commission example is one we will always aspire to emulate (Matthew 28:18-20). Thank you Russ for your example of spiritual multiplication (2 Timothy 2:2). The GCA would not exist if it hadn't been for your support. We love you and will always thank God for you and all you have invested in our lives and ministry.

Contents

Following Jesus

Discipleship Essentials

Introduction

A disciple is simply a person who follows Jesus, loving, obeying, and serving Him first and foremost. Jesus invited His followers to be authentic disciples (Luke 14:27). He also called all of His disciples to make disciples (Matthew 28:18-20). Growing into a disciple-making disciple of Jesus Christ is something that is exciting and a real privilege. This workbook will help you lay a strong foundation for an incredible lifetime of discipleship!

Notes on how to use this resource:

If you are going through this resource alone, work through each chapter with a focus on growing closer to God. Ask people you trust to help clarify any concepts you don't understand.

If you are going through this resource with another believer, make sure to take the initiative to encourage them with these principles. Meet together weekly to go over this material and discuss it together.

If you are going through this as a group, use this material as a conversation guide. Spend time working through the passages, but make sure to ask each other good questions as you go!

Once you have gone through this content, ask God to give you opportunities to encourage others with this resource.

For more information on how to use this tool in discipleship visit

https://www.greatcommissionalliance.org/discipleship.html

Understanding Your Identity in Jesus

LET'S START

Take a moment to discuss why you think confidence about identity is important. Share a story or memory when your sense of identity impacted you in the past.

How you view God, yourself, and the relationship between the two will impact every other aspect of your life. Jesus taught an important parable that tells us a lot about these important topics in Luke 15:11-32. It is the parable of the prodigal son. Take a few minutes to read Jesus' words below before diving into the rest of this lesson about your identity in Christ.

Luke 15:11-32 - "There was a man who had two sons. The younger one said to his father, 'Father, give me my share of the estate.' So he divided his property between them. Not long after that, the younger son got together all he had, set off for a distant country and there squandered his wealth in wild living. After he had spent everything, there was a severe famine in that whole country, and he began to be in need. So he went and hired himself out to a citizen of that country, who sent him to his fields to feed pigs. He longed to fill his stomach with the pods that the pigs were eating, but no one gave him anything. When he came to his senses, he said, 'How many of my father's hired men have food to spare, and here I am starving to death! I will set out and go back to my father and say to him: Father, I have sinned against heaven and against you. I am no longer worthy to be called your son; make me like one of your hired men.' So he got up and went to his father. But while he was still a long way off, his father saw him and was filled with compassion for him; he ran to his son, threw his arms around him and kissed him. The son said to him, 'Father, I have sinned against heaven and against you. I am no longer worthy to be called your son.' But the father said to his servants, 'Quick! Bring the best robe and put it on him. Put a ring on his finger and sandals on his feet. Bring the fattened calf and kill it. Let's have a feast and celebrate. For this son of mine was dead and is alive again; he was lost and is found.' So they began to celebrate."

1. Consider the father in this story; what does this parable teach you about the nature and character of God?

2. Consider the prodigal son in this story; what does this parable teach about God's heart for you and your relationship with God?

"Your real, new self (which is Christ's and also yours, and yours just because it is His) will not come as long as you are looking for it. It will come when you are looking for Him."
- C.S. Lewis
Mere Christianity

Walking with Jesus
Jesus uses the metaphor of a relationship between a father and child here. As we walk with God we learn to trust God as our Father!

Some of us aren't familiar with the concept of a loving father. If that is you, your heavenly Father is aware of how your earthly father has mistreated you. Your earthly father sinned against you and against God. That was never God's desire. Your heavenly Father is very different; He is the only perfect Father, and He desires to love, bless, and protect you. We'll use the analogy of a father in this workbook with the picture of your perfect heavenly Father in mind.

Imagine that as a child you were told not to play near a cliff but disobeyed, falling from the cliff onto a crumbling ledge, in risk of immediate death. Your best efforts only made the situation worse. Soon, your loving father arrived and lowered you a rope. You trusted him and grabbed the rope and were saved! Your faith was powerless on its own but enabled you to grab your father's rope and be saved. Once rescued you were safe in your father's love and confident of his forgiveness.

The father's rope is a picture of God's grace that saves you. Your willingness to trust the father is a picture of faith in Jesus. When we trust Him, He does for us what we could never do on our own. The father's forgiveness is a picture of God's mercy, His desire to forgive us. You have been saved by grace through faith and nothing can separate you from your heavenly Father's love (Romans 8:38-39, Ephesians 2:8-9)!

BIBLE TERMS

The word *Grace*, from the Greek word *Charis* (χάρις), means God's gift, blessing, or favor given to man through Jesus!

Key Concepts

Our sin separated us from God and we were destined for an eternity apart from Him. Thankfully, Jesus died for our sins and rose again that whoever believes in Him will be saved (John 3:16). You were forgiven and given the gift of eternal life when you put your faith in Jesus; now He has a wonderful plan for your life (Ephesians 2:8-10). You are His dearly loved child (Romans 8:15-16, Ephesians 5:1). That is your right as a believer (John 1:12), and nothing can change that or take that away from you. Jesus has an abundant life of meaning and purpose planned for you here on earth (John 10:10).

Have you believed in Jesus as Savior and Lord? If so, what is your story? If not, what would keep you from doing that today?

Read Ephesians 2:8-10

What did you have to do for God to give you eternal life? What will God do through you as you simply follow Him?

Read John 10:25-30

Who are Jesus' sheep? What can they be sure of? Who can take that away from them?

Read Romans 8:38-39
What does God promise you in this verse? Would He ever break His promise?

Read Philippians 1:6
Who started the good work in you? Who will finish it? Why does that matter?

Living It Out
Take some time to work on the story of how God rescued you. This will help you understand who you are in Christ and it will help you be ready to share your story with others when the opportunity comes up. Go to Appendix B to work on your rescue story!

Wrapping Up
Your heavenly Father loves you so much! Next week we'll learn about growing in our walk with Jesus. Until then, spend some time reading the Gospel of John. We know you'll get a lot out of God's Word as you spend time in it each day.

When you get a chance this week, take some time to read and study the following passages with the Inductive Bible Study Approach (Appendix A):
Psalm 139:1-18
John 1:12
Romans 8:1
2 Corinthians 5:17
Ephesians 5:1
Hebrews 12:1-2
1 John 5:11-15
Matthew 16:24-26

LET'S START

Who is the best friend you've ever had? Why was this person such a special friend? Have you ever felt close to God like that? Spend a few minutes discussing this.

Every person was created for relationship with God, but that relationship was broken by sin (Genesis 1-3). Jesus made a way for us to be forgiven and for relationship with God to be restored. When Jesus died on the cross, He paid the penalty for our sins so that whoever believes in Him will be forgiven and experience eternal life (John 3:16). Of course, eternal life in heaven is an exciting prospect, but the Christian need not wait for heaven to experience all that God has for them. Believers have been made right with God and have been given the right of being His children (John 1:12). That relationship is solid. Believers also have the opportunity to live in close friendship with Jesus each and every day. Here's something Jesus said about that.

John 17:3 - "Now this is eternal life: that they may know you, the only true God, and Jesus Christ, whom you have sent."

On a scale of 1 to 10 (with 10 being high) how would you characterize your walk with God today? Why did you pick that number?

How have you grown with God in the past? When has your walk with God been strongest? Why was that the case?

Key Concepts

As you continue growing closer to God, there are three big growth areas that will become apparent. These will be the foundation for the rest of this discipleship resource. These are your relationship with God, your relationships with other people, and your participation with God in what He is doing.

Having believed in Jesus, you have been adopted into His family (Romans 8:15). Your relationship with God was finalized when you put your faith in Him. As a child of God, you are now called to walk in close friendship and fellowship with Him each day (1 Corinthians 1:9, 2 Corinthians 13:14, 1 John 1:1-9). Spending time with Jesus in His Word and in prayer, spending time with other believers, and taking time to serve God are all important parts of spiritual growth.

"A rule I have had for many years is to treat the Lord Jesus Christ as a personal friend. It is not a creed, a mere empty doctrine, but it is Christ Himself we have."
- D.L. Moody
The D.L. Moody Collection

Read John 15:5

What does it mean to abide in Christ? What things do you think help cultivate deep fellowship with Jesus?

Read 1 Peter 2:2

How can God's Word help us grow in our walk with God? How should a believer prioritize God's Word as they grow with God?

Read Mark 12:29-31

What is the most important thing in life? What is the second? How can you grow close to Jesus in these areas? (1 Peter 2:2)

BIBLE TERMS

The word *fellowship*, from the Greek word *koinonia* (κοινωνία), means fellowship, association, community, participation, closeness, and intimacy!

Read Matthew 28:18-20

This is what has been called the Great Commission. How does serving God relate to fellowship with Him?

Walking with Jesus

As we walk with Jesus, we grow in a father and child relationship with God. Family relationships provide some insight into a few important truths.

A child is legally connected to his or her parents. When the child disobeys, there is no change in this legal relationship. However, there can be an effect on the fellowship or closeness the child enjoys with the parent. When the child asks the parent's forgiveness, their fellowship can be restored.

Similarly, your relationship with God is something that has been given to you because of what Christ did for you at the cross and your decision to believe in Him (John 1:12). Your salvation is not earned or kept through what you do or don't do (Romans 3:20). When you sin, confess that to God and know He will immediately forgive you and restore your fellowship with Him (1 John 1:5-9). Then ask Him to empower you by His Spirit to say no to sin next time! Realize today that you are God's child and He lavishes His love on you (1 John 3:1). Live each day as His dearly loved child!

Living It Out

In this session, we discussed growing close to God, growing in our relationships with other believers, and partnering with God in what He is doing around us. These are all important areas of growth, but they all revolve around the first one, our closeness with the Lord. Remember, Jesus said that apart from Him we can do nothing (John 15:5).

One important step of obedience Jesus has called His followers to is baptism (Matthew 28:18-20). There is a lot of confusion about this topic so we want to make sure to address it briefly here. Baptism is not a condition of salvation

14

(John 3:16, Acts 16:31, Romans 10:9, Ephesians 2:8-9) but an outward demonstration of the reality of what God has done in your life (Romans 6:1-7, Colossians 2:9-15). The believer should be baptized after believing in Jesus as Savior and Lord as a demonstration to the world that their past life is now gone and they have been raised a new person in Christ. Have you been baptized? If not, talk with someone who is encouraging you in your walk with God and make a plan to be baptized.

If you have already been baptized, refer back to your answer about where your walk with God is on a scale of 1 to 10. Considering what you listed, ask the Lord what next step He would have you take with Him. Write that below:

_____

_____

_____

_____

Wrapping Up

We hope you got a lot out of this lesson. Keep growing close to God by reading the Bible, praying, spending time with other Christians, and serving God as He leads you. Next week we'll learn more about spending time with Jesus on a daily basis. Until then, keep reading in the Gospel of John or one of the other Gospels in the New Testament. We know you'll get a whole lot out of God's Word as you take time to read it and study it each day.

When you get a chance this week, take some time to read and study the following passages with the Inductive Bible Study Method (see Appendix A):
John 13:34-35, 15:12
1 Corinthians 1:9
2 Peter 1:3-9, 3:9
1 John 4:19.

LET'S START

Why do you think spending time with friends is so important to relationships? Do you remember a time when someone you love made time for you? How did that affect your relationship?

Friends spend quality time together. Spouses spend quality time together. Family members spend quality time together. Spending time with people we love is a fundamental part of growing those relationships. It is no different with God. Spending quality time alone with God each day is a habit that leads to unparalleled peace and growth. It is a critical part of growing closer to God and following Him.

While Jesus walked this earth two thousand years ago, He was committed to spending quality time with God the Father. Jesus is fully God (Matthew 1:23, John 1:1). The Bible tells us that God is one God that exists as a perfect unity of three persons; the Father, Son, and Holy Spirit (Matthew 28:19). Three dimensional space is a great example of something that is one distinct essence comprised of three united parts. Although Jesus is fully God, He also demonstrated complete commitment to staying in close fellowship with God the Father on a daily basis. His example is a great one to follow.

Mark. 1:35 - "Very early in the morning, while it was still dark, Jesus got up, left the house and went off to a solitary place, where he prayed."

Jesus was committed to scheduling the first part of each day for uninterrupted time with the Father. How can we follow His example?

How do you think a habit like this could help you grow in your walk with God?

Key Concepts

Relationships always grow when friends spend time together. Your daily time with the Lord is not a duty; it is a great privilege to look forward to with joy and anticipation. It is a privilege to abide with Christ (John 15:5) spending time with Him throughout the day (remember David's example in Psalm. 1:1-3). There is no rule about how to do this. Simply remember that your relationship with God will grow more and more as you spend time with Him. Make it a point to schedule quality time with the Lord each day. Enjoy your times with Him, growing in praise, prayer, and God's Word.

> *"Ten minutes spent in the presence of Christ every day ... will make the whole day different."*
> *- Henry Drummond*

Read Luke 10:38-42

What is the one thing that matters? Why is this more important than other things that need to get done?

Read Luke 5:16

Jesus spent quality time with the Father in distraction free places. How can you follow His example?

Read Matthew 4:4

Most of us don't forget to eat; eating is part of a healthy daily routine. How could prioritizing God's Word in the same way we treat our meals each day impact a person's life?

BIBLE TERMS

The word *abide*, from the Greek word *meno* (μένω), means to remain with, stay with, wait with, continue with, and live with!

Read Philippians 4:6-7
What does this passage say will result from prayer? How does prayer help us grow closer to Jesus?

Walking with Jesus

Remember, Jesus loves you so much! God desires to love, bless, and protect you (Psalm 136). He also has designed you for an incredible purpose (Ephesians 2:8-10). As you spend time with Him, make sure to enjoy your fellowship with God rather than seeing it as a duty that you must fulfill. Your daily times with the Lord will help you grow close to Him and they will become a foundation for all the Lord will do in and through you! God loves you and desires to spend time with you!

Living It Out

Spending quality time with the Lord each day is critical to growing in your walk with Him. Consider how to make this a part of every day. Start by scheduling a time to do this each morning. List that below. Next, consider a good place with limited distractions to spend time with God. List that below too.

Time:

Location:

Don't feel like you have to achieve perfection! Don't think about where you want to be in this area ten years from now; simply take the step you need to take right now. Get your Bible, a cup of coffee or tea, and get ready for a special time with Jesus each morning. Keep doing this day after day and you'll soon come to treasure this habit as one of your favorite parts of the day!

Wrapping Up

We hope you got a lot out of this lesson. You'll grow tremendously as you cultivate a habit of spending time with the Lord on a daily basis. There will undoubtedly be days you miss spending time with Jesus. Don't panic; simply get back to your daily times with the Lord and keep growing. Next week we'll learn more about how to study the Bible. Until then, keep growing in your walk with God and keep helping others grow close to Him too!

GOING DEEPER

When you get a chance this week, take some time to read and study the following passages with the Inductive Bible Study Method (See Appendix A):
Psalm 1:1-3 and 119:105
John 15:5
James 4:8
1 Thessalonians 5:17.

Learning from Jesus by Studying His Word

Have you ever had a light bulb moment, an epiphany that literally changed your life? What happened?
How were you transformed by what you learned?

The Bible is the Word of God. In a world filled with uncertainty, God's Word provides a sure foundation for life and its truth transforms everyone who reads it. There is not a question you will ever ask nor a circumstance that you'll ever encounter that the Bible won't prepare you for. We can trust the Bible and we can live our lives based on what it says is true about us, God, and the world. Jesus claimed that His Word should be the foundation for our lives. Here's what He said:

Matthew 7:24-27 - "Therefore everyone who hears these words of mine and puts them into practice is like a wise man who built his house on the rock. The rain came down, the streams rose, and the winds blew and beat against that house; yet it did not fall, because it had its foundation on the rock. But everyone who hears these words of mine and does not put them into practice is like a foolish man who built his house on sand. The rain came down, the streams rose, and the winds blew and beat against that house, and it fell with a great crash."

What do you think it would look like to build your life on the foundation of God's Word?

Why is putting Jesus' Words into practice so important?

The taller you want to build a building, the deeper you have to build its foundation. Otherwise, the building will not last but will collapse under the pressures it faces. We are no different! Growing and thriving in life will always be directly proportional to the strength of your foundation on God's Word.

"As you study your Bible with the help of the Holy Spirit, and live out the truths that God reveals to you, you will discover new stability, strength, and confidence."
- Kay Arthur
Discover the Bible for Yourself

Key Concepts

The Bible is the very Word of God (2 Timothy 3:16) and it transforms us from the inside out (Romans 12:2). God's Word is true and trustworthy. Although critics will try to undermine it, it has stood the test of time. Fulfilled prophecy, archaeological evidence, the coherence of Scripture, the accurate translation of God's Word, and scientific statements throughout it show us God's fingerprints all over the Bible. You'll learn more about this in the BEST FACTS apologetics resource. God's Word is the unshakable foundation our lives should be built on.

Read 2 Timothy 2:15

Why do you think it is important to read and correctly study God's Word (Remember the Inductive Bible Study Method in Appendix A)? How can you cultivate a discipline of doing this each day?

BIBLE TERMS

Read Psalm 119:11

Memorizing God's Word, or hiding it in your heart, has many benefits. What benefit does David describe here? What others can you think of?

Read Psalm 1:1-3

Meditating on God's Word is simply the process of deeply thinking about and contemplating what you have learned in the Bible. What does David claim results from this? How could this practice impact your life?

Read James 1:22

Why is applying what we learn so important? Is there anything in Scripture that you feel God is calling you to put into practice (maybe sharing your faith, forgiving someone, giving to the Lord, or something else)?

Walking with Jesus

The Bible is not just a religious text, it includes the very words of God (2 Timothy 3:16, 2 Peter 1:20-21). As you read, study, memorize, meditate on, and apply God's Word, remember that this is a fundamental aspect of your relationship with your heavenly Father. None of us are where we want to be concerning God's Word; we all have room to grow. Don't beat yourself up about your past negligence in this area, simply walk in God's grace and choose to take steps with this going forward. God loves you so much and wants to communicate with you. Every time you read the Bible you are literally reading God's words for you.

Living It Out

Reading, studying, memorizing, meditating on, and applying God's Word are all vitally important parts of the Christian life. A great way to grow in these areas is to begin journaling during your times with Jesus each morning. The application for this week is simple. Buy a journal and begin using it in your daily devotional times. As you study God's Word, write down what God is teaching you. As you consider how to apply it, write down the action steps God leads you in.

Wrapping Up

Jesus claimed that His sheep, everyone who believes in Him, would listen to His voice and that He would protect them (John 10:25-30). We are faced with the decision to listen to Him or other voices every day. In a world of chaos, deception, confusion, and danger, following Him is the only way (John 14:6)! As we read, study, memorize, meditate on, and apply God's Word, we will experience Him in every circumstance we face.

Next week we'll learn about trusting Jesus and walking by faith. Until then, keep spending time with Jesus, growing in His Word, and letting Him lead you and use you in the course of your daily life!

GOING DEEPER

When you get a chance this week, take some time to read and study the following passages with the Inductive Bible Study Method (See Appendix A):
Matthew 4:4
Romans 12:2
2 Corinthians 10:5
2 Timothy 3:16
1 Peter 2:2
2 Peter 1:3 and 20-21

LET'S START

> Why do you think trust is so important in relationships? Have you ever had a friend you could trust with anything? How did that level of trust affect your relationship?

Trust and faith are foundational to the Christian life (Hebrews 11:6). Some people are confused about what faith really is. Mark Twain claimed that "faith is believing what you know ain't so." That sure isn't the Christian view of faith! Faith is quite simply trusting God and His Word. Jesus claimed that those who trusted Him would have His power to live the Christian life.

Luke 14:12 - "I tell you the truth, anyone who has faith in me will do what I have been doing. He will do even greater things than these, because I am going to the Father."

Why do you think trusting God and walking by faith is so important?

How have you seen God grow your faith as you've taken steps trusting Him?

If you want to get stronger, the last thing you do is order new muscles. Instead, you grow the muscles you already have by exercising them. This is exactly what happens with our faith as we apply God's Word in our lives!

Key Concepts

Every Christian has access to all the faith they could ever need through God's Word (Romans 10:17, 12:3, 2 Peter 1:3). The disciples asked Jesus for more faith, but He insisted that the faith they had been given, even if it was as small as a mustard seed, was sufficient (Luke 17:5-6). Elsewhere He talked about how a small mustard seed would grow into a large plant (Mark 4:31-32). We don't need to sit around asking for more faith but rather should focus on growing the faith God has already given us by applying the truth of His Word in our lives. This was something that was evident in the Thessalonian believers (2 Thessalonians 1:3) and something Paul expected of the Corinthian believers (2 Corinthians 10:15). As you continue learning and applying God's Word, your faith will continue growing!

"Your faith may be just a little thread. It may be small and weak, but act on that faith. It does not matter how big your faith is, but rather, where your faith is."
- Billy Graham

Read Hebrews 11:1

What is this passage saying about faith? If you really believe something, how will that impact how you live your life? If you really trust someone, how will that impact how you follow them?

Read Ephesians 2:8-9

What role did faith play in your salvation?

The word *faith*, from the Greek word *pistis* (πίστις), means belief, trust, confidence, and a conviction of the truth!

Read Romans 10:17

What role does God's Word play in regards to faith? What role does applying God's Word play?

Read 2 Corinthians 5:7

What does it mean to walk by faith? How can you walk by faith day by day?

Walking with Jesus

Our heavenly Father knows what is best for us and wants what is best for us. He also knows that when we stray from His will it always hurts us. Because He loves us, He invites us to trust His Word and follow Him by faith. Every relationship is built on trust, likewise walking by faith is critical to growing with God. This is also something that pleases God (Hebrews 11:6).

Remember what Jesus said about building on the foundation of His Word in Matthew 7:24-27? Well, let's revisit that. If we build our lives on the foundation of the truth of God's Word, we will experience peace and purpose. If we build on a shaky foundation of changing circumstances, fickle emotions, and finite perception, we will inevitably encounter chaos, disorder, and ruin. Our Father does not want that for us. He has given us His Word as a guide for our lives (Psalm 119:105). As we trust and walk with Him we will experience the abundant life He promises (John 10:10).

Living It Out

Have you ever seen a little child running and leaping off of a ledge into her father's hands? Her circumstances scream, "stop!" She undoubtedly feels safer perched in her safe spot. Looking down will inevitably terrify her. Yet, because her father has proven himself over and over, she knows the truth that she will be safe leaping into his loving arms. Every one of us goes through this same scenario day after day. The Lord has always proven Himself true, and His way always proves to be the best. Still, our circumstances, feelings, and perspective tell us not to trust Him. We must learn to trust Him and believe what He says is true.

What step of faith does the Lord want you to trust Him with right now?

What circumstances, feelings, and perspectives keep you from that?

How do you plan to trust Him, taking that step of faith, relying on Him like never before?

Wrapping Up

Walking by faith is fundamental to the Christian life. You'll have a million different thoughts about your value, identity, and purpose that conflict with what God says is true. By faith you'll have to remind yourself of the truth. You'll have friends, family members, and the society you live in tell you things that aren't true. By faith you'll have to remind yourself of the truth. There will be things you know God is calling you to that you don't feel like you can handle. By faith you'll have to remind yourself of the truth. Jesus has called you to a life of purpose and invited you to be a part of His Great Commission. This is what He was talking about in Luke 14:12. Walk by faith and trust Him to do what only He can.

We hope you've been encouraged as we've looked at walking by faith. Next week we'll be talking about experiencing Jesus' victory over sin. Until then, keep making time to spend reading the Bible each day. You'll grow tremendously as you cultivate a habit of spending time with the Lord on a daily basis.

GOING DEEPER

When you get a chance this week, take some time to read and study the following passages with the Inductive Bible Study Method (See Appendix A):
1 Corinthians 16:13
Galatians 2:20
Colossians 2:6-7
Hebrews 4:2
James 2:17-22

6

Experiencing Jesus' Victory Over Sin

LET'S START

Have you ever experienced the agony of defeat or the exhilaration of victory? Consider either experience and how it might relate to your walk with God.

Jesus has called us to be His disciples, followers who will believe His Word and yield to Him in every aspect of life, following Him in all He calls us to. Of course, we are all familiar with how often we fail to live up to that standard. Learning to follow Jesus is more about growing closer to Him than it is about trying not to sin. As we grow closer to Him and learn His Word, we will experience an internal transformation that transcends anything we could ever accomplish in our own strength (Romans 12:1-2). Here's what Jesus had to say about that.

John 8:31-36 - "To the Jews who had believed him, Jesus said, 'If you hold to my teaching, you are really my disciples. Then you will know the truth, and the truth will set you free.' They answered him, 'We are Abraham's descendants and have never been slaves of anyone. How can you say that we shall be set free?' Jesus replied, 'I tell you the truth, everyone who sins is a slave to sin. Now a slave has no permanent place in the family, but a son belongs to it forever. So if the Son sets you free, you will be free indeed.'"

What is the connection between knowing the truth and victory over sin?

What is the connection between knowing your identity as a child of God and victory over sin?

A team that only focuses on not losing will inevitably always loose. One that has its eyes on the prize will always do better. Similarly, if we're only focused on not sinning, we'll usually end up experiencing a lot of defeat. If we get our eyes on Christ and focus on growing closer to Him we'll experience more and more victory.

Key Concepts

You cannot fix your own problems by just trying harder. If you want to experience the Christ-like life God has called you to, you'll have to approach it in a radically new way. That starts with walking in God's grace and growing closer to Him, allowing Him to change you from the inside out.

James 1:15-16 tells us that sin follows temptation and that temptation is rooted in our desires. As God transforms our desires, temptation has less and less to work with. As we delight ourselves in God, He transforms our desires and changes our hearts (Psalm 37:4, Ezekiel 36:26). As we grow in His Word He transforms our thinking and our corresponding actions (Romans 12:1-2). If you want to experience victory over sin, draw near to Jesus and let Him work in you how only He can.

Read 1 Corinthians 10:13

As you continue growing closer to God, growing in His Word, He will continue transforming you from the inside out. You'll still have times, however, when temptation rages. What does this verse promise you? How will you rely on Him and apply this verse when temptation comes?

"Outside of Christ, I am only a sinner, but in Christ, I am saved. Outside of Christ, I am empty; in Christ, I am full. Outside of Christ, I am weak; in Christ, I am strong. Outside of Christ, I cannot; in Christ, I am more than able. Outside of Christ, I have been defeated; in Christ, I am already victorious. How meaningful are the words, 'in Christ.'"
- Watchman Nee

BIBLE TERMS

Read 1 John 1:5-2:2

Remember the difference between relationship and fellowship (see the *Walking with Jesus* section in lesson 2). When you confess your sin to the Lord, what effect does that have on the quality of your fellowship with your Father?

Read Romans 7:14-8:1

Have you ever experienced the struggle Paul describes here? What is Paul's hope for victory (7:25)? What is Paul's confidence in the battle (8:1)?

Psalm 103:12

As God's child, what does God do with your sin? How should that affect the way you live your life?

Walking with Jesus

It is easy to feel like a failure after falling. Remind yourself that God forgives you, is committed to you, and sees you as a new creation (2 Corinthians 5:17, Philippians 1:6). Agree with Him about that and experience victory over sin by walking close to Him, in His love, forgiveness, and grace.

Living It Out

Accountability is vitally important to Christian growth and victory over sin (James 5:16). Accountability partners are friends who will stand with us, pray with us, keep our struggles confidential, and encourage us in our battles with sin. Think of a mature, trusted Christian friend that you feel would be a good accountability partner. List their name below and plan a time to ask them if they would be willing to commit to being an accountability partner.

Name: _____

Wrapping Up

We wanted to wrap this session up with the VICTORY acronym, which we hope will encourage you in your battle with sin. Here it is:

1) Value victory! Remember that Jesus' way is always best (John 10:10).

2) Intentionally draw near to Jesus. Let Him change you from the inside out (John 15:5).

3) Cut off the hand that causes you to sin. Eliminate the things that trigger temptation and sin in your life (Matthew 5:30).

4) Take the initiative to deal with your past. Confess all known sin and don't let past mistakes drive your future (1 John 1:9).

5) Outline your escape route. Plan beforehand what you'll do when temptation comes (1 Corinthians 10:13).

6) Rely on the power of the Holy Spirit in your battle with sin (Ephesians 5:18).

7) Yell for help when you need it! Encouraging accountability is so helpful (James 5:16).

We hope this session equipped you with some practical steps for beating sin. Keep growing closer to Jesus, allowing Him to transform you. Next week we'll learn about the power of the Holy Spirit. Until then, keep spending time with Jesus and growing in His Word!

GOING DEEPER

When you get a chance this week, take some time to read and study the following passages with the Inductive Bible Study Method (See Appendix A):
Romans 12:1-2
2 Corinthians 5:17
Hebrews 12:1-2,
James 1:15-16,
2 Peter 1:3-4

7

Experiencing Jesus' Power

LET'S START

Have you ever felt like you didn't have what it took for something in your walk with God but somehow it all panned out? What happened? How did the Lord enable you to do what you knew you couldn't on your own?

The Holy Spirit is God (Genesis 1:1-2, Acts 5:3-4, 2 Corinthians 3:18). He is an important part of the Trinity (Matthew 28:18-20). He indwells believers and empowers them to live Christ-like lives. Jesus gave us the Holy Spirit and He enables us to follow God with God's own power. Every believer is given the Holy Spirit when they believe in Jesus, but many never experience the filling and power of the Holy Spirit that God desires to give them. The same Holy Spirit who worked powerfully through Jesus now lives in believers (Romans 8:11). The Christian life is not about trying harder but about learning to walk close to the Lord and in the power of the Holy Spirit. Listen to what Jesus said about the Holy Spirit.

John 16:7 (NASB) - "But I tell you the truth, it is to your advantage that I go away; for if I do not go away, the Helper will not come to you; but if I go, I will send Him to you."

Why does Jesus call the Holy Spirit our Helper? Note: some translations use different words here; the Greek word (παράκλητος) parakletos can mean advocate, intercessor, comforter, or helper.

Based on Jesus' words here, how important is the Holy Spirit?

Twenty Things the Holy Spirit Does for Believers

1. He reveals our sin to us to lead us to repentance (John 16:8).

2. When we believe in Jesus Christ as Savior and Lord, we receive the Holy Spirit (John 7:38-39, Ephesians 1:13).

3. At that very moment, He baptizes us into the Body of Christ (1 Corinthians 12:13).

4. He enables us to be adopted into God's family (Romans 8:15).

5. He guarantees our salvation (Ephesians 1:13).

6. In the Old Testament He would come and go, but now He lives in us (Psalm 51:11, John 14:17, 1 Corinthians 3:16, 6:19, 2 Timothy 1:14).

7. At salvation, He begins helping us become more and more like Jesus (Romans 15:16, 2 Corinthians 3:18, Titus 3:5).

8. He produces love, joy, peace, patience, kindness, goodness, faithfulness, gentleness, and self control in us (Galatians 5:22-23).

9. He guides us (Romans 8:14).

10. He encourages, comforts, and helps us (John 16:7).

11. He leads us into the truth (John 16:13-14).

12. He teaches us and reminds us of God's Word (John 14:26).

13. He gives us hope (Romans 15:13).

"To be filled with the Spirit means simply that the Christian voluntarily surrenders life and will to the Spirit. Through faith, the believer's personality is permeated, mastered, and controlled by the Spirit."
- J. Oswald Sanders
Spiritual Leadership

14. He enables us to understand God's Word and the things of God (1 Corinthians 2:12).

15. Ezekiel's story shows us how He enables us to obey God (Ezekiel 36:27).

16. He helps us pray (Romans 8:26, Jude 1:20).

17. He empowers us for bold evangelism (Acts 1:8, 1 Thessalonians 1:5, 1 Peter 1:12).

18. He helps us speak the words God wants us to speak (Mark 13:11, Luke 12:11-12).

19. He even gives all of us spiritual gifts that enable us to serve God and participate in His work in the church (Romans 12:4-9, 1 Corinthians 12:4-11, Hebrews 2:4).

20. Everything the Holy Spirit does glorifies Christ (John 16:14).

That's an incredible list! The Holy Spirit is very active in every believer's life. He also desires to fill every believer with His power on a continual basis (Ephesians 5:18). Being filled with the Spirit enables us to experience God's power in every area of the Christian life.

Imagine trying to push a car to get where you need to go. Hard right? Maybe even impossible! Imagine getting over a hill only to have the car speed down the other side out of control. Sound familiar? This is how many Christians do the Christian life, in their own strength. Compare that to simply turning the car on and letting the engine power the vehicle safely to its destination. That's what it is like to allow the Holy Spirit to empower your life rather than trying to do it on your own. The Holy Spirit is available to empower every believer to do what they could never do on their own. Unfortunately, so many people continue trying to live the Christian life in their own strength. Take some time studying the following passages to learn how to be filled with and empowered by the Holy Spirit.

Read John 7:37-39
What do you have to do to receive the Holy Spirit?

Read 1 John 5:14-15
Being filled with the Spirit is God's will for all believers (Ephesians 5:18). What can we be sure of if we ask Him to fill us with His Spirit?

BIBLE TERMS

The word *filled*, from the Greek word *plērousthe* (πληροῦσθε), means keep being filled. It is a present passive imperative verb meaning that this is to be an ongoing part of the Christian life. The passive voice also implies that this is something that the Holy Spirit does in us as we yield to Him, it is not something that we accomplish through our own effort.

....

....

....

....

....

....

....

Read Ephesians 5:18

God commands us to be continually filled with the Spirit. How can you intentionally be filled with the Spirit (remember, this is a continuing command meant to be ongoing, to keep being filled)?

Read Acts 4:31

What did the filling of the Holy Spirit empower these believers to do? Do you think He will do the same thing for you as you allow Him to fill you?

Walking with Jesus

Imagine your father was a billionaire with massive influence. No matter how weak you might be, your father's power would open doors for you everywhere you turned. In a similar way, we are truly weak on our own, but we are children of the God of the universe. When we surrender to Him, allowing Him to fill us and empower us with His Spirit, we experience His power.

Living It Out

Luke 4:1, Acts 2:4, 4:8, 31, 7:55, 9:17, 11:24, 13:9, and 52 describe numerous instances of believers being filled and empowered by the Spirit. The power of the Holy Spirit is available for us too. We can experience that as we surrender to Him and allow Him to fill us by faith.

Consider an area of your life that you have been struggling to obey God in. Maybe this is a sin of commission (like lust, hate, or pride) or omission (like not sharing your faith or not forgiving).

List an issue you're struggling with or need God's help in:

_____

_____

Now, consider the POWER acronym in relation to this issue. This acronym will help you remember a few keys to the Spirit-filled life.

1) Present yourself to God, surrendering this issue to Him (Romans 12:1-2).

2) Own up to your sin, confessing any sin with this issue to Him (1 John 1:9).

3) Want to honor God with this issue, choosing to live a Christ-like, Spirit-filled, and empowered life (Matthew 5:6).

4) Experience His filling and power concerning this issue, claiming it by faith alone through prayer (James 1:6-7, 1 John 5:14-15).

5) Rely on Him, taking a step of faith that requires Him to come through with this issue (2 Corinthians 5:7).

This is not a recipe for achieving power, but rather a reminder for how to surrender to Him receiving His power for all He calls you to. Remember the POWER acronym throughout your daily routines and ministry opportunities.

Wrapping Up
Make it a habit to live a Spirit-filled life asking God to fill you with His Spirit throughout each and every day. Remember to POWER up often! When you ask Him to fill you with the Holy Spirit you can know that He will, regardless of how you feel or what your circumstances look like. You can know that you will be filled with the Holy Spirit by faith alone, trusting that when you ask He will give you whatever you ask according to His will, as He has promised (1 John 5:14-15).

We'll be looking at prayer next week. Until then, keep prioritizing your time with the Lord and in His Word each day! Remember, you are a dearly loved child of God (Ephesians 5:1). Keep growing close to Him and allowing Him to work in your life.

When you get a chance this week, take some time to read and study the following passages with the Inductive Bible Study Method (See Appendix A):
Ezekiel 2:1
John 15:26-16:15
Acts 1:8
Romans 8:9-17
Galatians 5:22-23
2 Timothy 1:7

8

Talking with Jesus and Growing in Prayer

Have you ever had a long, heart to heart talk with a close friend? How did authentic communication build that relationship? What happens to relationships when there isn't that kind of communication?

Prayer is quite simply talking to God. God doesn't expect formalities here; He's after your heart. Prayer is not so much an avenue to getting things from God, rather it is part of growing closer to God. It is a natural result of faith in Jesus! Since I trust Him, I will be quick to talk to Him about what I'm going through. Jesus taught His disciples some key principles about prayer in a short little passage in Matthew. He emphasized coming to God with an awareness of His magnitude and praying in line with His will. He also described the importance of confessing our sin to Him and asking Him to meet our needs. Here's what He said.

Matthew 6:9-13 - "This, then, is how you should pray: 'Our Father in heaven, hallowed be your name, your kingdom come, your will be done on earth as it is in heaven. Give us today our daily bread. Forgive us our debts, as we also have forgiven our debtors. And lead us not into temptation, but deliver us from the evil one.'"

Why is it important to approach prayer with a correct view of who God is?

How can honoring God, confessing any known sin, and asking God to meet your needs grow you closer to God?

Key Concepts

Prayer is communication between you and God. You can pray silently in your mind. You can pray out loud. You can pray alone or with friends. You can pray for or about anything that comes to your mind. Prayer is not a spiritual button we press to get what we want; prayer is communication with God. God answers every prayer we ever pray. He doesn't always answer the way we want Him to, but He always answers the way that is in our best eternal interest. Prayer is critical to the Christian life, and it is a fundamental part of growing closer to Jesus.

> "Those who do not believe do not pray. This is a good functional definition of faith. Faith prays, unbelief does not."
> - John A. Hardon

Read John 14:13-14

What is Jesus' promise to us about prayer? What does it mean to ask something in Jesus' name?

Read 1 John 5:14-15

What does it mean to pray according to God's will? What can we be confident of when we pray according to God's will?

Read 1 Thessalonians 5:17

What does it mean to pray without ceasing? What could this look like in real life?

The word *father*, from the Greek word *pater* (πατήρ), literally just means father, but that is exciting! God implores us to talk to Him like we would to a loving father (Romans 8:15).

Read Philippians 4:6-7
What is the result of a vibrant prayer life? Would you like to experience this in your life?

Walking with Jesus

Jesus invites us to pour out our hearts to our heavenly Father. Children ask their dads for all sorts of different things. Sometimes their dads say, "Yes," other times, "Maybe," and still other times, "No." A loving father's answers are always made with the child's best interest in mind. The same is true of our heavenly Father (Matthew 7:7-11). Prayer is less about getting a "yes" and more about growing closer to our Father. Still, our Father loves us and desires to meet our needs. He wants us to talk to Him about everything that's on our minds.

Living It Out

No relationship can grow without authentic communication. Jesus does not want us to approach prayer as a religious obligation. God asks us to come to Him out of love, longing to grow closer to Him, as we pour out our hearts to Him on a continual basis.

One way to pray in line with God's will is to pray for lost friends and family members. God wants us to pray for all people and He wants all people to come to know Him (1 Timothy 2:1-4). A great way to remind yourself to be praying for friends and family members who don't yet know the Lord is to develop a top five prayer list. Ask God to help you think of five people He would like you to pray for on a daily basis. Then, list them and begin praying for them during your time with the Lord each day.

1. _____.

2. _____.

3. _____.

4. _____.

5. _____.

As you pray for these people, also ask God to give you opportunities to share with them, and then be ready to share when those come up!

Wrapping Up

We hope you learned a lot about prayer in this lesson. Remember, prayer is not a duty, it is a relationship. Talk to God knowing He is your heavenly Father who loves you dearly (John 16:26-27).

Next week we'll learn about growing closer to other believers! Until then, keep growing closer to the Lord and enjoying Him and your times in the Word and in prayer with Him.

GOING DEEPER

When you get a chance this week, take some time to read and study the following passages with the Inductive Bible Study Method (See Appendix A):
Matthew 7:7-8
Romans 12:12
Colossians 4:2
1 Timothy 2:1-4
James 5:13

9
Building Friendships with Brothers and Sisters who Love Jesus

LET'S START

Have you ever had a friend influence you in a way that changed your life? What was that like? If not, how could that have helped you?

Being a disciple of Jesus Christ is definitely a personal commitment, but it doesn't end there. Christians weren't meant to live the Christian life alone. We need each other to grow and thrive in our walk with God. We need Christian friends who will pray for us, encourage us, support us, and keep us accountable. Although your relationship with God is a personal one, you'll never grow very far in that relationship outside of a community of other believers. Jesus put a huge emphasis on this.

John 13:34-35 "A new command I give you: Love one another. As I have loved you, so you must love one another. By this all men will know that you are my disciples, if you love one another."

How can we love our brothers and sisters in Christ as Christ has loved us?

What impact will authentic, Christian love have on the world?

Walking with Jesus

As we grow in our relationship with Jesus, we must continue growing in our relationships with our brothers and sisters in Christ as well. God has made you a vital part of His family (John 8:35-36, Romans 12:4-5, Ephesians 3:14-19)! You need other believers and other believers need you!

Key Concepts

Although you can connect in a very personal way with God when you're alone with Him, you still need to grow authentic relationships with other believers. That happens best in Bible believing churches. We all need each other and will grow best in our walk with God when we don't neglect relationships with other believers. The Bible uses the metaphor of the body when referring to believers. The Body of Christ is a term that refers to Christians collectively. We all need to grow within this context of other believers. Just like a hand, foot, heart, or head needs the other parts of the body, we too need each other.

> "Real spiritual friendship is eagerly helping one another know, serve, love, and resemble God in deeper and deeper ways."
> - Timothy Keller

Read 1 Corinthians 13:4-8

This passage articulately defines selfless, Christian love. How can you allow God in you to love others this way (remember the power of the Holy Spirit!)?

Read Acts 2:42

What four elements characterized fellowship in the Church in Acts?

1.

2.

BIBLE TERMS

The word *love*, from the Greek word *agape* (ἀγάπη), means selfless, unconditional love that chooses others' good over one's own.

3.

4.

Read Hebrews 10:24-25

What are some of the key components of Christian fellowship in this passage? What does this tell us about the importance of being committed to growing in a local church?

Read Romans 12:3-10

Why do you need other believers? Why do they need you? How should we be devoted to each other in the Body of Christ?

Living It Out

We cannot thrive in our walk with the Lord if we live our Christian lives in isolation from other believers. No church is perfect and no Christian is perfect. If you try to find problems with a group of believers, you will inevitably find plenty. Instead of doing that, be committed to growing in the context of a group of Bible believing Christians.

If you don't yet have a local church, find a local church that is Jesus focused, Bible believing, and Great Commission pursuing and plug in! List your plan to find a local church below.

If you are involved in a local church, think of how you could take a step to grow closer friendships with believers in your church. List that below.

_____

_____

_____

Hopefully you are working through this workbook with a trusted friend or small group of friends. Make a plan to do something fun this week with that person or group of friends. Schedule your plan below.

_____

_____

_____

Wrapping Up

Loneliness and isolation have been associated with all sorts of negative physical and mental outcomes. People were not meant to live outside of community. Fellowship with other believers really is an important part of our walk with God. God will use other believers to grow us in so many ways. Authentic Christian friends can bring tremendous joy to our lives and can help us grow closer to Jesus. You're also probably aware that friends, even Christian friends, can hurt us! That will be the focus of the next session. Next week we'll learn how to practice forgiveness and protect our relationships with brothers and sisters in Christ. It will be an important session to say the least!

Until then remember that Jesus has called you His friend (John 15:14-15)! Keep growing closer to Him each day. He will continue growing you into the person He wants you to be as you simply focus on growing closer to Him.

GOING DEEPER

When you get a chance this week, take some time to read and study the following passages with the Inductive Bible Study Method (See Appendix A):
Mark 12:29-31
Philippians 2:1-11
1 Peter 4:10
1 John 1:5-9

10

Protecting Friendships with Brothers and Sisters who Love Jesus

LET'S START

Most of us have been hurt by someone we've loved in the past. The loss of a friendship can be painful. Have you ever had a broken relationship like that restored? What was that like? How is that relationship today?

The previous lesson discussed the importance of growing relationships with other believers. Since no one is perfect you'll inevitably encounter conflict and broken relationships as you do this. We need each other, but we also end up hurting each other from time to time. Don't let broken relationships with other believers turn you away from authentic fellowship. Learn to reconcile relationships quickly. Jesus taught that forgiveness is critically important.

Matthew 18:21-22 "Then Peter came to him and asked, 'Lord, how often should I forgive someone who sins against me? Seven times?' 'No!' Jesus replied, 'seventy times seven!'" (NLT)

What is Jesus telling Peter about forgiveness in this passage?

Considering how God has forgiven us, how should we forgive others who have hurt us?

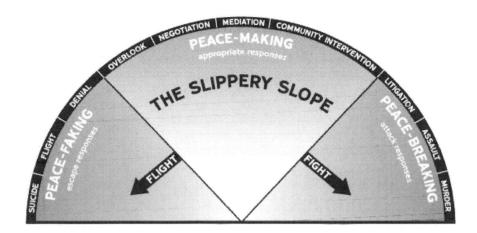

Ken Sande's Peacemaking grid above, from his book The Peacemaker, is very helpful. It describes healthy, biblical, peace-making responses to conflict as well as unhealthy peace-faking and peace-breaking responses. Are you more likely to slide to one side of this spectrum or the other? How do you think God would have you grow as a peacemaker?

"Forgiveness is the key which unlocks the door of resentment and the handcuffs of hatred. It breaks the chains of bitterness and the shackles of selfishness."
- Corrie Ten Boom

Key Concepts
People you love will sin against you. Christians you look up to will at some point let you down. No church is perfect and even great churches will sometimes hurt people. Resolve to live at peace and reconcile relationships. There is tremendous joy in forgiveness but ongoing grief and pain in unforgiveness. In fact, forgiveness is often one of the first and most significant steps towards healing from past wounds.

Read Colossians 3:13
What is God's Word telling us about forgiveness? How should Christ's example motivate us in this?

BIBLE TERMS

The word *forgive*, from the Greek word *aphiemi* (ἀφίημι), means to let go, to give up a debt, to leave behind, and to forgive.

Read Matthew 7:3-5

What should our perspective be when it comes to those who have wronged us? How might this change how we reconcile with those that we have hurt or who have hurt us?

Read Matthew 18:15-17

What should you do if you've been wronged by a brother or sister in Christ? Why is it important to do reconciliation this way rather than reacting against the person with gossip, slander, and rage?

Read Matthew 5:23-24

This passage makes it clear that we shouldn't go on with life and serving God while maintaining unresolved conflict. What should you do if you remember that you have wronged a brother or sister?

Walking with Jesus

It isn't easy to forgive people when they have hurt us. Sometimes it is even harder to ask people we've hurt to forgive us. These are fundamental parts of the Christian life. When we forgive others, we let go of how they have hurt us and don't require them to make it right. This doesn't mean that we condone the wrong that they have done, instead, we trust the Lord with the situation and surrender our bitterness to Him. Doing this leads to incredible healing in our lives. Refusing to do this leads to bitterness and pain.

48

Living It Out

Do you have a broken relationship that needs to be restored right now? Do you need to forgive someone that has hurt you? Do you need to ask someone you have hurt to forgive you? Describe how you'll handle these situations below (refer to appendix C for help on this).

_____

_____

_____

_____

Wrapping Up

This is an intense lesson to work through for most people. Forgiveness is not easy, but it is important. Here are a couple last thoughts on this.

First, forgiveness does not necessarily equal trust. If you've been hurt deeply and repeatedly, you should still forgive. You should also be careful to set up good boundaries to keep yourself from being hurt more in the future. If this is your situation, please talk to a spiritual leader you trust about this.

Second, be careful with passages like Matthew 6:15 (Jesus was speaking to Jews bound by the Old Testament law not believers saved by grace). You have been saved by grace through faith. Unforgiveness is a fellowship issue not a relationship issue! Confess it as sin and allow your fellowship with the Lord to be restored. Then, forgive those that have wronged you going forward.

Third, be quick to overlook offenses (Proverbs 19:11). When we are offended, we have the choice to become angry and bitter, or to love others and give up keeping a record of wrongs (1 Corinthians 13:4-8). Instead of assuming their motives and believing the worst, seek to overlook offenses and believe the best about others.

Next week we'll discuss evangelism and sharing Christ's message of forgiveness with others. Until then, keep forgiving others and keep growing closer to Jesus knowing He always forgives you!

GOING DEEPER

When you get a chance this week, take some time to read and study the following passages with the Inductive Bible Study Method (See Appendix A):
Matthew 18:21-35
Luke 7:47
1 Peter 4:8

11

Telling Others the Good News About Jesus

LET'S START

What is the best news you've ever heard? How did that impact your life? Were you excited to tell people the great news?

The Good News of what Jesus has done for us is too good to keep to ourselves. All believers have the incredible opportunity of helping people around them learn about Jesus and all He offers them. This is a privilege the Lord Himself gave to His followers. We have also been promised the power of the Holy Spirit to enable us to bring the Good News throughout the world. Here's what Jesus promised concerning that.

Acts 1:8 - "But you will receive power when the Holy Spirit comes on you; and you will be my witnesses in Jerusalem, and in all Judea and Samaria, and to the ends of the earth."

Do you think Jesus really intended for His followers to be His witnesses to the ends of the earth? If so, why do you believe this and how do you think this applies to your situation?

How can you rely on the power of the Holy Spirit in evangelism (refer back to lesson 7)? Note: evangelism comes from the Greek word for good news and simply means telling others the Good News of Jesus.

Farmers know that they will never reap a harvest if they don't first plant seeds, and their harvest will always be proportional to the amount of seed sown. In a similar way, we are called to share the Gospel with people everywhere knowing that some of them will respond and come into a relationship with Jesus. Conversely, if the Gospel isn't preached, people won't come to faith in Jesus.

"Three-hundred-million years from now, the only thing that will matter is who is in heaven and who is in hell. And if that is the only thing that will matter then, that should be one of our greatest concerns now."
- Mark Cahill

Key Concepts

All Christians have the great privilege of telling others about Jesus and the Good News of the Gospel. We also have the promise of the power of the Holy Spirit for this work. We are not alone. Sharing our faith is an exciting part of the Christian life, and it is one that is eternally significant as well.

Read Matthew 4:19
What did Jesus tell His first disciples? Do you think the same privilege is ours today? How should evangelism flow out of following Jesus?

Read Matthew 9:36-37
What was Jesus' attitude about the lost? Why does Jesus use the metaphor of a ripe harvest? What is the limiting factor: the problems in society or the lack of Christians willing to share their faith?

The word *gospel*, from the Greek word *euaggelion* (εὐαγγέλιον), literally means good news.

Read Romans. 10:13-15
Why should we share the Good News? What will happen if we don't?

Read Colossians. 4:5
What are some of the opportunities you encounter on a regular basis? How can you make the most of them for the Gospel?

Walking with Jesus

Telling others about Jesus will come naturally if our hearts are passionate about Him. Jesus told us that the mouth speaks from what is treasured in the heart (Matthew 12:34). As believers, we have been invited by God to partner with God in what He is doing (1 Corinthians 3:7-9). That is an honor and a privilege! Get excited about joining God in His work and growing closer to Him as you serve Him and tell others about Him!

Living It Out

What Jesus has done for us is truly good news, and there is no other way people can be saved (Acts 4:12). The Gospel really is the power of God for salvation (Romans 1:16). The core elements of the Gospel are God's love, humanity's sin and the consequence of separation from God, Jesus' solution, and our choice to believe in Him or not. God doesn't want anyone to perish (2 Peter 3:9), and He wants everyone to be saved (1 Timothy 2:4). He has called each of us to be a part of reaching the lost with His Good News (Acts 1:8). We have been entrusted with the task of sharing the Gospel with others. That is a privilege!

One great way to share the Good News is to share your testimony. Go to Appendix C and work through Oasis World Ministries' One Minute Witness worksheet. You might want to refer back to your answers from the application section of lesson 1 (found in Appendix B).

Refine this and spend some time practicing your testimony. Next week you'll have the opportunity to go out and use your story in evangelism. Spend time between now and then prayerfully preparing your heart for God to use you!

Wrapping Up

Sharing the Gospel is an incredible privilege. Think about it, you get to partner with God in what He is doing in someone else's life in a way that will make a difference for all of eternity! We hope you'll decide today to join God for the rest of your life in the incredible work He is doing around the globe!

We hope you were encouraged to share your faith by this week's lesson. Start taking steps of faith to tell others what God has done in your life. Keep it simple and enjoy the privilege of partnering with God in His work in other peoples' lives. When Satan lies to you about all the reasons you shouldn't share your faith, remember the truth of God's Word and the fact that it is a privilege to tell others about your hope in Jesus!

Next week will be a big week. You'll have a chance to take a step of faith and share your faith! Take time this week to grow close to God allowing Him to prepare you for next week's adventure.

GOING DEEPER

When you get a chance this week, take some time to read and study the following passages with the Inductive Bible Study Method (See Appendix A):
Matthew 13:1-23, and 28:18-20
John 3:16
Acts 17:26-27
Rom. 1:16
1 Corinthians 3:6
2 Corinthians 5:11-21

12

Tell Others What Jesus has done in your Life

LET'S START

How do you feel about going out and sharing your faith?

Take a deep breath and trust God with whatever is going on in your mind and heart right now. You will get through this. Evangelism is something that seems to scare almost everyone. If you're feeling a little anxious about today, don't worry, you're not alone. Most of life's greatest adventures and biggest decisions include a little bit of fear as well! Get excited. God is going to work in your life and in others' lives today. That is a fact!

Mind Check

Some of the following misconceptions have sidetracked many before you. Check any of these misconceptions that have sidetracked you before. If you want to compare these misconceptions with what God's Word says, check out the scripture references in parentheses at the end of each statement.

☐ "Preach always, use words if necessary," (Romans 10:13-15).

☐ "You must have the gift of evangelism," (Matthew 4:19).

☐ "Your personality, style, and knowledge make the Gospel relevant," (1 Corinthians 1:27).

☐ "You must earn the right to be heard," (John 3:16).

☐ "Evangelistic resources and tools don't work," (Romans 1:16).

☐ "Only the destitute need Jesus," (1 Timothy 2:4).

☐ "All is lost if someone gets offended," (Matthew 10:22).

☐ "Methods are what produce results," (Matthew 13:1-9).

☐ "Older people aren't interested," (John 12:32-33).

☐ "Most people aren't interested," (Matthew 9:37).

Heart Check

So we've dealt with a few misconceptions. Now, even more importantly, let's look at our hearts. Before taking another step, evaluate where your heart is at. In Matthew 12:34, Jesus said, "Out of the overflow of the heart the mouth speaks." Evangelism should be the natural expression of a heart that is set on Jesus. Take a moment to surrender your heart to the Lord and to put Him in His rightful place of authority in your life.

Strength Check

Remember Acts 1:8, which says, "But you will receive power when the Holy Spirit comes on you; and you will be my witnesses in Jerusalem, and in all Judea and Samaria, and to the ends of the earth." Because the Holy Spirit lives in you His power is available to you at every single moment in your life. All you need to do is to consciously choose to surrender to Him, asking Him to fill you and empower you for His will! Remember the POWER acronym and consider it as you prepare to share.

1) Present yourself to God, surrendering to Him (Romans 12:1-2).

2) Own up to any sin concerning evangelism (1 John 1:9).

3) Want to honor God by sharing the Good News with the lost (Matthew 5:6).

"Success in witnessing is simply taking the initiative to share Christ in the power of the Holy Spirit and leaving the results to God. The only way we ever fail in our witness is if we fail to witness."
- Bill Bright

4) Experience His filling and power claiming it by faith (James 1:6-7, 1 John 5:14-15).Take a minute to pray right now and ask God to fill you and empower you with His Spirit. He will empower you no matter how you feel. Trust Him!

5) Rely on Him and take a step of faith (2 Corinthians 5:7)! Now, go for it! Practice your one minute witness (in Appendix C) one last time with a friend and then go out to a public place and spend at least 30 minutes sharing your faith using this tool.

Destination:

Departure time:

Return time:

Debrief. Take a few minutes to review what just happened.

How many people did you get to talk with?

What were some of their responses?

What were your highlights?

56

What were some of your disappointments?

What did you learn?

What would you do differently next time?

You did it!!! You made it through an awesome time of evangelism. It will only get better from here. You can be sure that God will keep working in the lives of the people you shared your story with.

Living It Out

Refer back to the Top 5 list you wrote down in lesson 8. Consider how you might share your testimony with each of them.

Wrapping Up

You are off to a great start. Most Christians will never take the step of faith that you just took today. Please don't stop here. Continue allowing God to use you by stepping out in faith, in the power of the Holy Spirit, and sharing your faith each and every day!

Next week we will wrap up this workbook looking at the amazing purpose Jesus has created for you. It will be exciting. Until then, take some time to enjoy God. Spend some time with Him and reflect on what He has been doing in and through your life during this season.

GOING DEEPER

When you get a chance this week, take some time to read and study the following passages with the Inductive Bible Study Method (See Appendix A): Read John 4:28-30 and 39-42. Consider the power of this woman's testimony and how God can use our testimonies in a similar way.

13

Experiencing the Amazing Purpose Jesus has for You

LET'S START

Have you ever felt like you were doing exactly the right thing in exactly the right place at exactly the right time? What was that like?

God has designed you for a life of meaning and significance (Ephesians 2:8-10). An abundant life of purpose is something that Jesus promised to those that follow Him (John 10:10). This week we'll look at some of the general aspects of God's incredible purpose for your life. One grand theme of your purpose is the Great Commission we'll begin with that passage.

Matthew 28:18-20 - Then Jesus came to them and said, "All authority in heaven and on earth has been given to me. Therefore go and make disciples of all nations, baptizing them in the name of the Father and of the Son and of the Holy Spirit, and teaching them to obey everything I have commanded you. And surely I am with you always, to the very end of the age."

Considering how you have grown as Christ's disciple, how do you think you could help others become His disciples too?

What role does evangelism play in making disciples?

Fruit trees always produce more fruit when they are pruned correctly. Jesus has designed you to experience an abundant life that makes an impact for Him, and He will continue pruning your life so you'll be more fruitful. He will use the circumstances you experience to prune you to be maximally effective and full of joy in Him (John 15:1-11). Although this process can be painful at times, it always leads to greater good and more fruitfulness (Hebrews 12:7-11). As you grow in your faith, commit to growing closer to the Lord, knowing He will do a great work in and through you (John 15:5).

Key Concepts

This passage in Matthew 28 is one that presents an exciting vision of the potential that awaits every believer. None of us are called to live mediocre lives devoid of impact. God desires that you would live a life of significance that would be focused on loving Him, loving others, glorifying God in all you do, and making disciples. Making disciples begins with evangelism, but it goes beyond that as well. Now that you have been through this workbook, you could walk through this with a younger believer helping to disciple them!

Romans 12:1-2

What three things does this passage call us to? How does God's Word relate to renewing our minds and being transformed? What is the promise here for those who follow God in these areas?

"The Great Commission is not an option to be considered, it is a command to be obeyed."
- Hudson Taylor

BIBLE TERMS

The word *go*, from the Greek verb *poreuomai* (πορεύομαι), is in the middle voice meaning as you are traveling, going, pursuing, journeying, and following. In other words, whatever you do in life, do it with a Great Commission focus!

Read 1 Timothy 4:12-16

What does Paul implore Timothy to do here? How can you follow Paul's challenge to Timothy as you consider the next steps God has for you?

Read 2 Timothy 2:2

This passage describes spiritual multiplication; the process of making disciples who will make disciples, who will make disciples. If you began multiplying like this once each year, and the next believers you discipled did too, the whole world would be reached in less than 40 years! How do you think you could begin making disciples like Paul told Timothy to? How will you continue growing in discipleship as you begin making disciples?

Read Revelation 7:9-10

This passage shows a picture of people from every nation, tribe, people, and language worshiping God in heaven. The Great Commission will be completed some day. How can you live your life with the vision of the Great Commission in mind?

Walking with Jesus

You are God's dearly loved child and that is the foundation for a life of following Him and serving Him (Ephesians 5:1). As we conclude this workbook, please remember that everything we've talked about should flow from intimacy with God (John 15:5), not a sense of obligation.

Living It Out

God has called you to a life of close fellowship with Him. He has also designed you for peace and harmony with other people. Incredibly, He has even invited you to partner with Him in His plan for the world! As a believer you can now walk in joy and peace as you step into the life of meaning, purpose, and significance God has planned for you.

You've undoubtedly grown a lot as you've worked through this workbook. This is by no means the end! In fact, it is really just the beginning. We know God has great things in store for you. As we bring this workbook to a close, we want you to spend a little time thinking about the next steps God is calling you to.

What next steps is God calling you to in your walk with Him (Mk. 12:29-30)?

What next steps is God calling you to in your relationships with others (Mk. 12:31)?

What next steps is God calling you to within the context of the Great Commission (Mt. 28:18-20)? See the Funnel diagram in Appendix E.

Wrapping Up

As you consider these next steps, remember the importance of walking in close fellowship with the Lord. Our fellowship with Jesus is our first priority (Luke 10:38-42, John 15:5). Keep growing closer to Jesus and ask Him to help you share your faith and make disciples!

GOING DEEPER

When you get a chance this week, take some time to read and study the following passages with the Inductive Bible Study Method (See Appendix A):
Psalm 96
Matthew 25:14-30
Acts 1:8
Ephesians 2:8-10

Summary

You've reached the end! Way to go! Remember, following Jesus is a lifelong journey so the end of this workbook is really just the beginning.

Remember to love God with all your heart, mind, soul, and strength and keep loving your neighbors as yourself (Mark 12:29-31). Make it your ambition to pursue Jesus, glorifying Him in all you do (1 Corinthians 10:31). Keep making disciples that will make disciples that will make disciples (Matthew 28:18-20, 2 Timothy 2:2).

Keep spending time growing in and being transformed by God's Word (Romans 12:1-2). His Word is the foundation for our lives. Please be careful to guard against the lies that will hit you from every direction. You might want to review Appendix F for a list of things that are dead giveaways for deception. Keep growing in prayer, pouring out your heart to God (1 Thessalonians 5:17)! Keep fellowshipping with other believers (Hebrews 10:24-25). Keep sharing your faith (Acts 1:8)! Ask God to help you go through this resource with a younger Christian.

Whatever you do, keep following Jesus! You'll hit obstacles and roadblocks, but He will never leave you nor forsake you (Hebrews 13:5).

Appendix A

The Inductive Bible Study Method

First, ask God to give you wisdom and to guide you. God will give you wisdom when you ask (James 1:5), and the Holy Spirit will shed light on His Word for you (1 Corinthians 2:12). Then, follow these three steps.

Observation

Consider the big picture. Ask who, what, when, where, why, and how questions. Who was this written to? What was the setting? What was being addressed? What is the context of the passage? What are some of the key elements of the passage? Are there key words that come up throughout this passage? Are there key people? Are there any contrasts or comparisons being made? Try to outline as many key observations as you can about the passage before moving on. Resources like studylight.org and blueletterbible.org are helpful online tools.

Interpretation

What is the core meaning of this passage? Consider the big picture observations you just made. Look at the rest of Scripture. You might do a word search to see what other verses have to say about what you're studying. Use Scripture to interpret Scripture. This is especially important when interpreting Old Testament passages; consider the New Testament context. Check to see if the Old Testament passage you're reading is mentioned in the New Testament. Look at the meanings of the words that are used. After all of this, try to understand the core meaning of the passage. You might check commentaries that are included with resources like studylight.org and blueletterbible.org to see if you're on the right track.

Application

Finally, remember James 1:22 and ask God to give you wisdom about how He would have you apply what you have learned.

Appendix B

Your Story

As you consider who you are in Christ, remember where He has brought you from. We'll revisit this later but for now, keep it simple.

A. What three words describe your life before Christ? If you trusted Christ at a young age, what words describe some of your weaknesses apart from Christ.

1) _____, 2) _____, 3) _____

B. How did you come to faith in Christ? Briefly mention the key aspects of the Gospel here (God's love, your sin, Jesus' provision, and your decision to trust Him).

C. What three words describe your life since trusting Christ? Be honest as you share the great work He has done and is doing in your life.

1) _____, 2) _____, 3) _____

Appendix C

The Communication Wheel

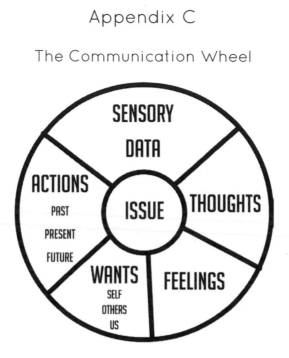

How to use the communication wheel. Role play through this a few times to get comfortable with it.

Communication Wheel definitions
These may seem selfish, but it is important to express what we think, feel and want.

Issue: Define what's at the heart of the issue. Use "I" statements. Own the issue.

Sensory data: Explain what you took in from your senses.

Thoughts: Describe what you thought and interpreted.

Feelings: Use "feeling" words, like sad, lonely, frustrated, ect.

Wants: Say what you want for yourself, others, and each other.

Actions: Discuss past actions (what caused the issue), present actions and future actions (specific things you would like to see happen).

Communication Wheel directions

>Each person should go through the whole wheel until completely finished and then switch. You can go in any order. Jump back and forth, etc.

>If possible write out the wheel ahead of time.

>Let the other person make their point and be respectful about not interrupting. Ask questions when it is clear that there is a good point to do that.

Follow these rules (James 1:19):

Seek to understand. It takes supernatural power to put your needs on hold and try to understand the other person (Pr. 18:2). Most conflicts are resolved when you understand each other.

Speak for yourself. Use "I" statements. Take ownership of your feelings. Try not to accuse or blame.

Listen by following. You want to hear their story. Asking leading questions makes you the leader; instead, follow where they go. Do not try to jump in and fix them or relate your autobiography. Just listen. Invite them to tell you more. Don't stop until they tell you they're done. Usually by the third time they'll begin to open up.

Listening tips:

Attend: establish eye contact, non-verbals.

Acknowledge: use agreeing statements (uh huh, right, etc).

Invite: ask them to tell you more.

Summarize: capture the essence of what they are saying in an empathetic way.

Appendix D

The One Minute Witness

The one minute witness is an Oasis World Ministries tool. Find out more about Oasis at oasisworldministries.org.

1. Begin by asking permission.

    a. Ask: "May I ask you a question?"

    b. If they say "Yes," ask, "What is the best thing that has ever happened to you?"

    c. Listen to them, converse with them, and show them you care. Then, when they are done, ask, "May I share the best thing that's ever happened to me?"

    d. If they say "Yes," continue with your one minute witness.

2. B.C. ~ Describe your life before Christ.

    a. Begin with, "There was a time in my life when," and then continue with three words or phrases that describe your life before Christ. Review your answers in appendix B and adapt as needed.

    1) _____.   2) _____.   3) _____.

3. T.P. ~ What was your Turning Point?

    a. How did you hear about Jesus? Again, review your answer in appendix B and adapt as needed. Don't forget to include the key elements of the Gospel (God's love, your sin, Jesus' provision, and your decision to trust Him).

    b. Now, share what you just wrote, and conclude with this, "When I realized Jesus died for my sins, I...,"

4. A.D. ~ Describe what Christ has done in your life.

    a. Begin with, "Since I met Jesus, I..." and then continue with three words or phrases that describe the change Christ has done in you (antonyms to the previous three can be good). Review your answers in appendix B and adapt as needed.

    1) _____.   2) _____.   3) _____.

5. Conclude with, "If I had never met Jesus..."

    a. Briefly summarize what your life would look like without Christ in one concluding sentence.

Those are the five elements of your one minute witness.

Now, POWER up and ask the Lord to fill you with His Spirit.

Then, take a step of faith and go out and meet people and start with, "May I ask you a question?"

If they say, "Yes," proceed with the next questions and your one minute witness.

Once you share your story, ask the person you are speaking with if they would be interested in knowing how Jesus could do something like this in their lives. If they say, "Yes", be prepared to go through the Gospel in more depth.

You might want to use the *Knowing God Personally* booklet, the Romans road, the God Tools app, or some other tool for this.

When you're through, ask them if they are ready to put their faith in Jesus Christ as Savior and Lord. If they are, lead them in a short prayer, helping them verbalize their decision to the Lord.

If someone you share with puts their faith in Christ, schedule a time to meet with them in the coming week for coffee and to encourage them in their new walk with God. You could bring them a Bible at that appointment. You could also start going through this workbook with them (just get them their own copy).

The Funnel Diagram

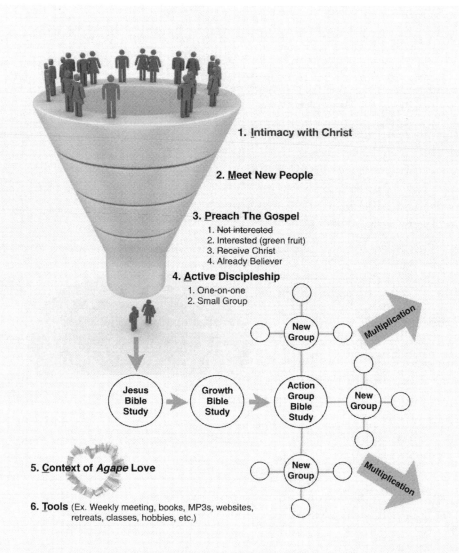

1. **Intimacy with Christ**

2. **Meet New People**

3. **Preach The Gospel**
   1. ~~Not interested~~
   2. Interested (green fruit)
   3. Receive Christ
   4. Already Believer

4. **Active Discipleship**
   1. One-on-one
   2. Small Group

Jesus Bible Study → Growth Bible Study → Action Group Bible Study → New Group

New Group — Multiplication

New Group — Multiplication

5. **Context of *Agape* Love**

6. **Tools** (Ex. Weekly meeting, books, MP3s, websites, retreats, classes, hobbies, etc.)

Appendix F

22 Warning Signs

Here are common signs of false teaching:

1. False teaching often attempts to predict the return of Christ (Matthew 24:23-24, 36, 50, 25:13, Mark 13:32, Luke 12:46).

2. False teaching is often overly preoccupied with signs and wonders (Matthew 24:24, 7:21-23, 12:39, 16:4).

3. False teaching is often motivated by personal desires (Romans16:18).

4. False teaching often uses flattery (Romans16:18).

5. False teaching often uses empty arguments aimed at the naive (Romans16:18, Ephesians 5:6, Colossians 2:4).

6. False teaching often distracts from simple and pure devotion to Christ (2 Corinthians 11:3),

7. False teaching often promotes foolishness (2 Corinthians 11:19-20).

8. False teaching often involves physical roughness (2 Corinthians 11:19-20).

9. False teaching often promotes legalism and manipulation (2 Corinthians 11:19-20, 1 Timothy 4:1-7).

10. False teaching often takes advantage of people (2 Corinthians 11:19-20).

11. False teaching often has hidden, secret, or unique teachings and "special revelation" (Colossians 2:18, 2 Peter 2:1-3).

12. False teaching often promotes speculation and fruitless discussion (1 Timothy 1:3-7).

13. False teaching often distracts people from doing God's work by faith (1 Timothy 1:3-7).

14. False teaching is often evidenced by confidence without understanding (1 Timothy 1:3-7).

15. False teaching often promotes myths and stories which differ from sound doctrine (1 Timothy 1:3-7, 2 Timothy 4:1-5).

16. False teaching is often accompanied by hypocrisy and acting like people did before Christ (1 Timothy 4:1-7, 2 Peter 2:17-22).

17. False teaching often goes from bad to worse (2 Timothy 3:13).

18. False teaching often makes Christianity look bad (2 Peter 2:1-3).

19. False teaching is often accompanied by greed and materialism (2 Peter 2:1-3).

20. False teaching often appeals to peoples' carnal desires and emotions (2 Peter 2:17-22).

21. False teaching is often evidenced by pride (2 Peter 2:17-22).

22. False teaching often promises freedom beyond God's Word (2 Peter 2:17-22).

Brandon and Anne Cox
(far left) helped with content organization, illustrations, and editing. The Coxes have been in ministry since 2013. Anne runs logistics for the GCA, while Brandon runs the next generation area of ministry.

Nate and Erin Herbst
(middle left) helped with content writing. The Herbsts have been in ministry since 2004. Erin (M.A.) is the assistant team coordinator and Nate (Ph.D) is the team coordinator.

Chris and Michelle Kachuriak
(middle right) helped with content organization and illustrations. The Kachuriaks have been in ministry since 2017. Michelle helps the ministry with compassion ministries and meeting practical needs, and Chris is focused on international partnerships and training.

Ben and Meghan Renfro
(far right) helped with content organization, illustrations, and editing. Meghan also did the graphic design. The Renfros have been in ministry since 2015. Meghan is the graphic designer, and Ben is in charge of technology and helps lead the church consulting and church planting support areas of the ministry.

NOTES

NOTES

NOTES

NOTES

NOTES

NOTES

NOTES

NOTES

NOTES

NOTES

NOTES

NOTES

NOTES

NOTES

Made in the USA
Columbia, SC
20 November 2018